Abuse

Healing and Recovering from the Trauma of Emotional Abuse Caused by Parents and Relationships

Table of Contents

Chapter 5: Further Tips and Exercises to Help

Conclusion

Introduction

I want to thank you and congratulate you for downloading my book, *"Abuse: Healing and recovering from the Trauma of Emotional Abuse Caused by Parents and Relationships."*

Alcohol, substance, physical, and emotional are various types of abuse someone can suffer from whether it is a parent or loved one who is causing the pain. You may inflict the pain on yourself by drinking too much or using drugs to ease the pain. You can also suffer from someone else creating pain, whether it is emotional or physical.

Our world does not focus enough on emotional abuse and the trauma that arises from this type of situation. Instead, the court systems around the world, including in the US, are set up to only assess physical trauma as a type of abuse.

Unfortunately, many children living in troubled homes face emotional abuse every day, doing their best just to survive, feeling that no one has the power to stop it. Even with clear evidence of emotional trauma caused by a parent or both parents, the legal system rarely intervenes because the laws are not strict enough to make it happen.

If you have suffered emotionally due to a parent or a past relationship, you know you must seek information to help you heal and recover from the trauma.

It will take strength. You may experience setbacks. But, in the end, you are already on your way to recovering and healing from the trauma of emotional abuse because you are seeking information to help you.

The information in this book is broken down into categories, with specific tips to help you, and exercises to help you work through your situation.

Whether your parents divorced, and one always yelled at you or around you, or worse disparaged the other parent, you will find ways to move past these experiences. If your parents (or stepparents) called you stupid, worthless, loser or otherwise whittled away at your self-esteem—you can find your way to a healthy life.

Thanks again for downloading this book, I hope you enjoy it!

Chapter 1: Exploring Emotional Abuse

Emotional abuse can happen to anyone: children, teens, or adults. Even strong people, with a proper upbringing, and solid foundation of confidence can enter into an abusive relationship. When someone is finally free of the abuse, they understand something was wrong, but during the period of emotional trauma, it can be difficult to see there is another choice besides just accepting what is happening to you.

Just because there is no physical mark does not mean there was not a problem, or a crime committed. It just means most law enforcement agencies are not willing to work as hard to help you prove the trauma and make it stop.

As such, emotional abuse is an elusive subject. However, despite the fact that it can sometimes be invisible to the outside world, emotional abuse can leave deep scars on a person's mind. The problems that arise from such experiences can fester and become more complicated over the years, causing further emotional issues that can manifest themselves in a number of ways and places. The relationship between the abuser and the victim may not always be where the damage ends.

Those who go through abuse and fail to properly address the problem and let go of the emotional weight can carry it over to their children. If kept suppressed inside and allowed to fester, emotional harm can almost become like a disease that's passed down through the generations. Folks can thus find themselves lashing out, not knowing how to express their love, and being unable to communicate with their children on a meaningful level. Before you know it, you can end up disparaging, neglecting, or otherwise scarring your children because of your own deep-seated, unaddressed problems.

Therefore, if you have ever been a victim of emotional abuse, it is imperative that you fully understand what it is, why it happens, and how you can overcome the problems it has left you with. No matter how difficult it might be to identify and mend the problem, you can and must do it not only for your own sake but that of your children and other loved ones.

Defining Emotional Abuse

Psychology texts define emotional abuse as any act that isolates, confines, verbally assaults, humiliates, or diminishes one's dignity, identity and self-worth. This psychological abuse is chronic, leading to low self-confidence, personality changes, depression, suicide and anxiety.

It's imperative that you understand that arguments, breakups, divorces and brutal honesty, especially when responding to a question, are not emotional abuse. All of these things can cause us varying degrees of stress and emotional pain, but they hardly equate to abuse.

If you have an argument with your parent or a partner, you need to analyze the situation and identify the underlying cause of the argument. If there is a well-defined, concrete issue at the center of an argument, then this is an unfortunate but normal human interaction, as disagreements are sometimes unavoidable. Furthermore, needless to say, if you ask for someone's opinion and you don't like what they have to say, you aren't being abused.

There are other situations in life where lines can get rather blurry. For instance, shouting is often an integral part of verbal and emotional abuse, yet not all shouting is abuse. We sometimes yell at each other to accentuate our point of view, because we are momentarily angry, or simply because we care. The difference between these familial moments and actual abuse is that, after the outburst, we are able to sit down, talk and resolve our issues, and the hurt we may have felt at the time will dissipate.

Another important thing to note when yelling is involved is the object of the verbal outburst. If your parent or spouse is yelling about a particular issue between you or a certain action you took that offended them, then this is merely their expression of dissatisfaction.

On the other hand, when the shouting involves deliberately hurtful words directed at your character, this is bordering on emotional abuse. As such, you need to differentiate between a verbal assault and an expression of rage – between an intention to harm and an intention to voice one's opinion. Abuse also frequently revolves around intimidation, so verbal threats are almost exclusively a mark of emotional abuse. Overall, abusers want to control and undermine you while upset loved ones want you to address the issues that set them off.

Examples of Emotional Abuse

The following are examples of emotional abuse provided by various sources, including psychology textbooks:

If a person intentionally frightens, threatens violence, abandonment or fear of no food or proper care, it is a sign of abuse. Lying to the child or adult or asking for the person being abused to lie is also an example of this type of abuse.

When a person is socially isolated, it is a sign and example of abuse. If relevant information is withheld and other information is made up or discussed inappropriately someone is suffering from abuse. Any defamation and slander of another is abuse.

Talking about death, to make someone do something, such as, "I'll kill myself if you leave me or do not comply with my wishes" is emotionally abusive. Telling someone they are not worth the trouble or too much trouble as well as ignoring or criticizing the person excessively is another example.

Trying to control a person, with unreasonable demands, treating a child like a servant or an adult like a child is emotional abuse. Being disrespectful or overly familiar can also be abusive.

Signs that a Person is Abusive

If a person yells, swears, bullies, or uses name-calling, insults, mocking, intimidation or threats, these are signs of abuse. Any ignoring, excluding, isolation, humiliation or denial of the abuse and projecting onto the victim are also signs of abuse.

The abuser may feel guilt and overcompensate for the abuse, but it is a cycle, so the pattern of abuse will appear again, with excessive makeup times, as well as plenty of excuses. The abuser tends to be charming, giving and apologetic which helps the abused feel their partner is genuinely sorry. Situations are set up so that more emotional abuse can take place until, eventually, the victim is stuck in the cycle, accepting the behavior or feeling that it is due to their own faults.

It's also important to understand that accidents or a genuine, temporary loss of control can indeed happen, especially among people who spend their entire lives together. Life gets difficult, the going gets tough, and none of us are impervious to frustration. If your parent or another loved one lashes out at you on one occasion and you know for a fact that this is unlike them, then you should be careful not to misinterpret such incidents as abuse, especially if they genuinely apologized and showed remorse. This can happen to any of us and it's much different to actual abuse, which is almost always systematic and, as mentioned, has a pattern.

If such an incident occurs once or reoccurs on rare occasions, another good way to differentiate it from abuse is by seeing if it's possible to talk about it with your loved one. In a normal, healthy relationship, it should always be possible to openly discuss any unpleasant incident such as a fight or a misunderstanding. A partner or parent who isn't abusive will want to hear out your grievances and take an objective look at themselves while taking your perspective seriously. When we tell our loved one that they hurt us by lashing out, for instance, they should be understanding, apologize, and take concrete steps to ensure it doesn't happen again.

On the other hand, an abuser will usually instantly get defensive, dismiss your grievances as "drama" or "weakness," and just generally deny that they did anything wrong whatsoever. After that, it's only a matter of time until it happens again, and you can rest assured that an abuser will defend his or her actions each time, acting like you are in the wrong or even trying to make you feel guilty.

Attacks on Your Self-Esteem and Potential

Abusers frequently suffer from low self-esteem. It's not uncommon at all for emotionally abusive individuals to see in their partners or children all those things they hate about themselves. These flaws may or may not be in you, but an abusive parent or spouse will see them nonetheless and go out of their way to point them out and use that as a line of attack against your character.

For instance, abusers who feel weak can label their child or spouse as such and constantly call them out on it, slowly chipping away at their character and confidence. If the abuser has significant influence over the victim, the subject might come to believe these accusations over time. Abusive parents who feel incompetent in one capacity or another will sometimes systematically attack their child for being the same even if the child shows promising talent or ability. The child can and will be convinced after enough repetition, ultimately destroying their potential.

It's a terrible thing for a parent to do to their child, but it happens all too often, whether or not it's on purpose. By the time the child has grown and come to fully understand their parent, it can already be too late. This is because he or she may not be strong enough to reverse the effect of all those abusive years, let alone make up for the lost time that could have been spent pursuing a particular dream or honing a skill that their parents convinced them they don't have. Even if they understand that their parent was merely channeling their own frustrations, these children may never go back to pursuing the dreams they were discouraged from.

This is why it's important to rely on yourself as much as possible and disregard naysayers, even if they are your own parents. However, make sure you don't confuse abusive discouragement with constructive criticism. Parents, partners, and people who genuinely care about you will tell you, for your own good, when your idea is bad or you're doing something wrong.

A non-abusive person who has your best interest at heart will explain in detail why they think you shouldn't do something, and they will recommend alternatives and try to help you. As always, you should look for patterns. If every single one of your ideas or dreams is constantly shot down with no constructive explanation, then this is likely a systematic way of undermining your character and potential.

This kind of abuse can also take on an even more sinister, deliberate form, especially in relationships and marriage. While parents are often unaware of what they are doing through their lack of support, spouses can be envious. Some abusers make it their mission to prevent their partners from achieving that which they personally failed at. For instance, abusive individuals who feel unaccomplished in a certain field or have seen their dreams crushed in the past may deliberately discourage their partner from pursuing their own success therein.

This is because such people can feel so hurt by their past failures that the idea of someone else succeeding makes them feel like even more of a failure, even if that someone is their partner. An inability to emotionally and genuinely partake in their loved one's happiness and success can be a result of low self-esteem or a general lack of empathy. Either way, envy takes over instead of compassion and congratulations, and sabotage can occur instead of support. This abusive behavior is perhaps even more frequent between friends, but it occurs between partners and spouses way more frequently than it should.

As before, patterns and rational are what gives the abusive behavior away. Committed loved ones will provide support initially and have your back through many failures. Your partner will compassionately and carefully give you their honest opinion only after it becomes clear beyond a reasonable doubt that your efforts are misguided and wasteful. Abusers who want you to fail, on the other hand, will never give you a modicum of support to begin with.

Recognizing the signs of emotional abuse and some examples will help you understand that, as the victim, it is not your fault. Let's use an exercise to determine if you are in a situation of emotional abuse.

Exercise to Recognize Emotional Abuse

- How often does a parent or partner call you names, such as stupid, loser, dumb, worthless?

- How often are you restricted from seeing friends?

- How often are you allowed to go out, only because the abuser in your relationship allows you to go?

- Do you catch your parent or partner in a lie? How often? What are the excuses and does the person try to backpedal when they are caught in a lie?

- How often do you feel ignored or criticized?

- Is the person disrespectful in public, as well as at home?

- Do you feel you are ordered around, told you are child-like or treated less than you are?

It takes time to look at these situations with an objective eye. Most victims do not like to think they are victims and it can take a long time for you to admit that you were or are. The adage "hindsight is 20/20" is true. When you are finally free of the abuse, it is easier to see it and find examples.

Psychology does not have a set rule for "frequency" of abuse. However, abusers typically begin slowly with the abuse occurring only occasionally, until the cycle becomes a monthly, weekly and then a daily occurrence.

When unchecked, an abuser can begin to send messages or make derogatory statements on a daily basis, with fewer and fewer apologies in between. However, this can also depend on the psychological issue that may be underlying this abusive behavior.

Abusers tend to have traumatic childhoods, where parents had the same emotionally abusive qualities, abused drugs or alcohol, or ignored the child altogether. It is not an excuse and should not be used as a way for the abuser to avoid facing their demons, but it is often a place to start—to understand why they are the way they are, so you can move on and know it was not your fault. You can finally accept that the person or parent had psychological issues affecting their behavior and they projected those on to you.

Chapter 2: Parental Abuse

Parental abuse can include abuse by grandparents, guardians, step-parents and anyone who has the authority to make decisions for a child. For example, if a grandparent came for a visit and made comments to their grandchild about how fat they are, or other comments regarding their physical appearance, it may not seem like abuse because it happens infrequently. However, derogatory statements still constitute abuse. The grandparent is not trying to help the child gain confidence but is taking it away.

Offhand, hurtful comments and remarks such as the ones mentioned are one of the instances where abuse doesn't necessarily require a pattern from one person. Children can be particularly sensitive to such things and they can affect them if they occur one too many times, whether or not the person who threw the comment is the child's regular abuser. In fact, the more individual people that pass a certain remark, the more of an effect it can have.

Children with weight problems and other similar issues are especially vulnerable in that regard. Sometimes, their parents aren't careful enough and their children can be exposed to hurtful, unconscionable comments from relatives at family gatherings, for instance.

Even worse is when it comes from a parent or step-parent that has a chance to berate and belittle you on a daily basis.

Unrestrained Criticism as Unintentional Abuse

Constant belittlement can be directed at a wide range of your personal traits, ranging from character to behavior to physical appearance.

It is truly sad just how frequently this abusive interaction can occur between parents and their children, but worse yet is how complicated the cause and the goal of such abuse can be. Namely, parents who berate or insult their child with the sole intention of causing harm are, of course, very rare and disturbed individuals. If you find yourself under an onslaught of weekly or daily hurtful comments relating to your behavior, character, or aspects of your appearance that can be changed, you need to consider the underlying cause of your parent's behavior. The chances that your parent hates you are incredibly slim.

In the simplest terms, their hurtful remarks are quite likely the result of sheer incompetence. For instance, if you have some extra weight or develop certain unhealthy habits, your parent's belittling comments might just be their way of expressing that they care about you and are concerned about your health and wellbeing. To be sure, this is a harmful and ineffective approach to parenting, but, unfortunately, insults and harshness are the only approach some parents know. In fact, it's likely that their parents too used insults and harsh remarks to get them to change their ways and get on the right track, never teaching them the virtue of support, kind words, and positive reinforcement.

This is where a line between constructive criticism and verbal abuse is crossed and significant emotional damage can be inflicted, so belittlement is still abusive, whether or not the parent is aware of what they're doing. However, what this means is that there is a possibility of talking to your parents about it and explaining how you feel. Even the most ignorant and clueless parents might be able to see the error of their ways if their child explains that the remarks are hurtful and make you feel low and unmotivated. After all, this will show them just how counter-productive their approach is, and they might understand that the way to move forward is to support you and help you rather than just hurl insults at you.

At the very least, understanding that your parents fundamentally wish you well can help you cope with their abusive ways. No child should have to endure verbal attacks, of course, but, sometimes, a change in perspective can function as a shield, help you overcome difficulties, and even become motivated. If your parents really care about you and just want to see you do better, then proving their insults wrong through action should certainly make them regret being hurtful.

This change in perspective can be especially helpful if the abuse you wish to overcome is already a thing of the past. If you suffer because you are unsure if your parents ever loved you due to all the hurtful words they threw at you on a daily basis, then understanding their perspective can help you alleviate those doubts. At the end of the day, even if they are abusive and hurtful in their remarks, most parents are just concerned about their child and they simply don't know any better.

The best way to identify whether or not your parents insulted you in an effort to motivate you is to reflect on how they behave after the object of their criticism has been corrected. If they commend you and the abuse never reoccurs, then they most likely just wanted you to do better. On the other hand, truly abusive parents will always find something wrong with you. When you respond and fix what they want you to fix, they will invent a new flaw in you, and the cycle will continue all your life. After a certain point, it becomes quite clear that the fault is not with you.

Examples of Parental Emotional Abuse

1. Calling the child fat or anorexic.
2. Ignoring the child.
3. Telling the child their grades are poor when they are not.
4. Not allowing a child to visit a friend because they do not like the friend or parents of that friend—this is isolation and combined with other things can be emotional abuse.
5. Isolating the child from the other parent, or never allowing them to be alone together.
6. Taunting the child.
7. Controlling what the child does or is allowed to say, without reasonable reasons. For example, being forceful or threatening, and not allowing the child to express their feelings and thoughts if they are not what the parent wishes to hear.
8. Being told you are stupid or will amount to nothing.

For instance, a child should be able to love both parents. However, in an emotionally abusive situation, the child may fear expressing their love for one parent because it hurts the other parent or causes anxiety/fear with the reaction the abusive parent has.

Emotional abuse can also involve the other parent, whether in a relationship or a divorce. Any time a child feels they cannot love both parents equally-that they are in the middle of adult issues or are disparaged for showing kindness, love, or other healthy emotions toward the other parent, this is an example of emotional abuse. If a parent walks in the door, ignores the child or children running over for affection, and continues to ignore their children's needs—it is abusive.

An entire book can be created around examples of parental emotional abuse. The above provides a look at some common situations that children face.

Other Causes of the Parent's Reaction

You understand you suffered from emotional abuse or still do. But, why does your parent feel the need to act this way? Are they just mean, disinterested, and just should not have become parents? Do they hate you, rather than love you? Are they in the right, and do you actually deserve the defamation, derogatory, and painful comments or lack of love?

Never. You never deserve the abuse you suffer. However, to help you heal and put less emphasis on the negative aspects of your childhood and overcome the trauma, you need to understand your parent and why they subjected you to such negativity and trauma.

Parents who abuse their children often have emotional or physical trauma themselves. But not all abusers come from damaged homes. Sometimes there is no apparent reason for the action of others. In addition to what we already discussed, the underlying causes of abuse can be as variable as people and their individual characters are.

For example, a parent who works and has no time for their children may not feel their behavior is traumatic, but to the child it is. The abandonment of the parent for work; especially, if the family has enough money without working 80 hours or more a week, is difficult. Workaholics by choice are not as easy to understand for a child because there is no "excuse" for the lack of love. The parent often does not realize how damaging it is for the child, but later, when the child is an adult and grievances are aired, the parent-child relationship can often be healed and the trauma dealt with versus being a hindrance for emotional well-being.

To explore this situation, consider a child who feels they are always second to their older sibling. Anger gets suppressed, and there is trauma as a result of being ignored that can manifest itself as an adult. Later on, the child may realize the parent didn't behave this way intentionally, and that the parent may have felt that not speaking about the child in front of them was the proper thing to do. While this example of unintentional abuse is traumatic, the damage can be repaired as the child begins to see their parents as a human being with flaws rather than having an expectation of parents who love unconditionally and never act in a way that might make them question that.

Parents who have their own scars as a result of trauma, on the other hand, leading to psychological issues, are harder to accept. A few reasons emotional abuse may occur in this case include:

1. Narcissism
2. Depression
3. Bipolar disorder
4. Other personality disorders
5. Emotional scars leading to a number of other disordered ways of thinking

If you suspect your parent has a psychological disorder, it can be easier to accept their behavior as not relating to you directly. A narcissist is someone who puts themselves first, always, even when they are trying to appear "selfless." They are controlling, verbally abusive and blame their behavior on others.

You might be inclined to think that narcissism is just a character flaw that can easily be corrected, but narcissism can take the form of a deep psychological disorder that can have a variety of causes. These causes are often rooted in childhood and upbringing, which means they frequently go back to your grandparents.

On the flipside, apart from being self-absorbed and self-centered and despite all of their vanity, narcissists often suffer from low self-esteem at the same time. This is the main reason why they fly off the handle so easily when criticized or somehow obstructed in their goals. The narcissist can take even the slightest criticism, no matter how logical and constructive, as a major attack on his or her character, which can have explosive consequences.

Narcissists are also almost always very envious and can wish failure upon other people, even their children. Their manipulative nature puts no limit to their attempts to use others for selfish gains and, in extreme cases, narcissistic parents will use and manipulate their children as well.

A person suffering from depression often tries to make the subject of their abuse feel as sad and underconfident as they do. However, in other situations, the depressed parent may just experience lethargy and a lack of interest rather than extending their behavior to verbal abuse.

Unfortunately, clinical depression is a very real disease that can take on extreme forms. The neglect that a clinically depressed parent can inflict upon their children can be immense, but this is one of the few instances where the parent is hardly to blame. Such a lack of interest and ability to cope with life can lead to tragic outcomes for the whole family, which is why clinical depression is something that must be treated by professionals, often with the help of medication.

Bipolar disorder is like a roller coast, where the person can be extremely happy and loving, and suddenly have a switch flip inside them, after which they may become lethargic, disinterested and verbally abusive toward you. Bipolar disorder is also known as manic depression, and it is usually categorized as a psychotic rather than a personality disorder.

Much like depression, this is a very serious condition that can have devastating consequences on the child, the suffering parent, and the family as a whole. While the disease is characterized by mood swings, a bipolar person will simply be depressed most of the time. The manic episodes, from which it gets its other name, will come occasionally and involve all sorts of erratic behavior, not just happiness and euphoria. Some patients will go through uncontrollable frustration and anger as well. The intensity of these episodes depends on the severity of the case.

Other personality disorders can include multiple personalities, in which case their behavior toward the child may differ wildly. This is because those who suffer from this disorder have their mind split up into different identities or personalities that are often switched uncontrollably. Generally known as dissociative identity disorder, this condition is all too real, no matter how unbelievable it might sound. Such individuals can lose all control of their actions and even their thoughts, which is very dangerous to everyone involved.

However, this and other disorders may also encompass anxiety disorders, which may cause the person to have their sense of certainty invalidated, leading to them wanting others to feel the same way, even their children. Anxiety often accompanies other psychological and personality issues. Apart from uncertainty, people suffering from anxiety often have a difficult time coping with stress as well as stressing over non-issues. Anxiety is also manifested as uncontrollable, persistent dread or fear of anything from judgment to physical harm, even when no such dangers exist. Constant stress, lashing out and having other outbursts are well-known marks of this condition.

Another issue that often leads to anger, disregard and other unscrupulous conduct is the antisocial personality disorder. This is not to be confused with social anxiety, as antisocial individuals are usually more than savvy in social situations. The problem is that they have no empathy or regard for other people and their needs, resembling the traits of a psychopath or sociopath. A sense of responsibility and commitment is something that antisocial people struggle with, which almost always impacts their children in a profound way.

Emotional instability and the breakdown of familial relationships also often accompany borderline personality disorder. This is usually the result of abuse, often sexual, suffered in one's formative years. People who suffer from this disorder generally have a deep fear of abandonment. That fear affects their relationships and self-control, which leaves such people prone to all kinds of outbursts. Those who threaten others with self-harm or suicide as a means of getting their way frequently suffer from the borderline personality disorder.

Keep in mind that these are merely brief introductions into some of the disorders that unstable and abusive parents can suffer from. The information can be used to provide small hints, but things are often more complicated. It is best to seek a counselor, therapist, or trained psychologist to help you pinpoint the cause of your parent's emotionally abusive behavior. You should not try to diagnose your parent, parents, or yourself.

You may think you know what is wrong with your parent, but find a professional opinion differs from what you thought.

Accepting Your Parent

Human nature demands that we understand the problem in order to move on from it. Acceptance is not going to come once a label is applied to your parent or abuser. You are not going to wake up suddenly and say, "I accept you for being a narcissist and all the trauma you subjected me to."

Time is the healer of wounds. Yes, it becomes possible for you to accept the parental behavior when you understand there is an underlying cause. However, you also must realize your parent is not going to apologize for their actions—not genuinely—unless they are receiving psychological assistance.

Acceptance is about looking at the other person and believing these statements, "My parent cannot help their behavior until they accept they have a problem. I understand their emotional or physical trauma, and I am free to interact or not with this person. If I choose to be a part of their life, I will take their statements at face value, and I will not believe what they say about me. I will not take the abuse, but excuse myself from it, and know I did my best."

You, even as a child still dependent on your parents, have the right to decide if you will subject yourself to their abuse or not. Children, who are unable to get away from the abuse and still desire love, often act accordingly and then use compensatory techniques to repair their self-confidence.

Exercise to Heal from the Trauma

Children and adults need coping mechanisms. However, children often require different techniques because they are still developing. If you have accessed this information because you wish to help a child suffering from emotional abuse, then you will want to follow those guidelines.

Helping Children Adapt

Children will often feel like they are put in the middle of two parents divorcing- especially if one parent is emotionally abusing the child. Even if it is not an instance of divorce, but rather of one parent abusing the child due to depression or other psychological problems, there are coping mechanisms that can help.

As a parent or adult in a child's life who is suffering from emotional abuse, you need to be very careful of what you say, how you say it, and what help you offer. You need to avoid putting a child in the middle, where they feel like they cannot love the parent causing the trauma. The best thing you can do is offer the child some mechanisms for dealing with the abuse, as well as assuring them you are always willing to listen.

1. Provide the child with a blank notebook. This journal is for the person to write their feelings, good or bad, as an outlet for those emotions. Often, because a child will worry that someone will see it due to a lack of privacy, they are hesitant to accept the notebook. However, you can offer a safe place to keep it and allow them access to it whenever they need it.

2. You do need to promise not to look at it, but only if you can keep that pledge. Your resolve may weaken because you want to know what is going through the person's mind. However, it is a huge violation to go through a

journal unless you have permission. So, do not break any promise you make regarding the information shared in the notebook. Or, even better, offer them even more security by offering both a secure location and a lock on their journal to which only they have the key.

3. Listen—the biggest thing you can do is listen. Listening is different from hearing. Listening takes an active role. You remain silent, interjecting words only when necessary, but always remembering what is said. Hearing is knowing the words, yet not truly comprehending what the person is saying. A child will not necessarily be devious, but just like any person may still hide emotions behind the words they say (or have trained themselves to say). So, it is your job to listen to the words and body language of the child you are trying to help.

4. When you offer advice, it should be with clear motives of helping the child. For example, you can begin by saying "I want to help. This is my opinion or these are the facts and if you feel uncomfortable or already know what I'm trying to say, then you can tell me, and I'll stop." By using these words, you provide the child with a way to say they do not want to listen or talk right now, but you also show you are capable of being there whenever they are ready.

5. Most people are not trained psychologists. Therefore, you should not act like one to a child. However, if you have the power to make decisions for the child or a way to help a parent supply counseling, make sure the abused child is getting the help they need from a professional.

6. Depending on the age of the abused child, they may or may not have solid reasoning skills. But, there is always the ability to develop them. Younger children require quicker tasks, designed to keep their mind engaged in the topic versus something like adults use in situations of abuse, anxiety and fear. Older kids can use methods similar to adults. You will need to choose the activity and coping mechanisms based on the age.

Children can express their feelings through drawings, acting silly, being too hyper or saying they are bored but interested. For example, a young ten-year-old was off listening to music and singing by herself. However, she was compelled to find out what her aunt and grandma were up to. Upon hearing that they were having an "at home spa day" where one was cutting her fingernails and the other her toenails, the child said, "It sounds boring."

The key is that the child didn't leave. When it came time to use paraffin wax on the adult's hands to help moisturize the skin and make them soft, the child was very interested and wanted to "try" it. Boredom was mentioned because the child wasn't asked to participate and secondly because she didn't know what it would entail. Yes, the adults were trimming their nails on their own, but the adults would also trim her nails and even allow them to be painted as part of the special spa time.

This kind of relaxed and open atmosphere between the mother and aunt who are also friends, and are sharing similar interests and involving the child can be the perfect kind of environment for a child suffering from abuse to begin to open up. The sharing of feelings, fun and a relaxed atmosphere can provide a way for everyone to share and relax instead of feeling estranged or pressured, and can allow children the opportunity to talk about things that are bothering them, rather than putting them on the spot and having them feel like you are demanding answers they don't know how to give.

You never want to have backhand statements, be too blunt without explaining your words, or make the child feel they must answer any question you ask. That is just adding to the trauma rather than helping the child feel safe and like they can trust you as they open up to you.

Parental Abuse—You Can Escape It

As an adult who suffered from parental abuse as a child, you have other ways of coping or escaping from the trauma. The information here is designed to help you move on from your childhood and accept that you cannot change your parent or what happened, but you can cope better throughout the rest of your life. You are always going to carry your emotional baggage: even when you want to let it go, it can rear its ugly head and take a bite out of your healthy mindset. However, you do not have to let it rule everything or even ruin relationships.

1. Seek a psychologist. There is a stigma that someone getting help from a psychologist, counselor, therapist or psychiatrist is mentally unhealthy, but do not fall into this mindset. It is untrue. You do not have to have any mental disorder to need someone you can trust to talk to. Yes, friends should be trustworthy, but they are not beholden to the same legal constraints about disclosure as a therapist. Your counselor cannot share anything with someone else. It ensures that your feelings, thoughts and emotions are safe and free from judgement, similar to how a young child can use a journal secured by a trusted adult as an outlet. Except in this case, you can actually receive feedback and advice on how to improve your mindset and heal your

trauma. Friends may judge or even talk about things you said with others without meaning to hurt you.

2. As someone who has suffered emotional abuse, you need to trust someone, to speak and to heal. An outside opinion, without any bias in the situation, can help you see more than one side. A wise person once said, there are often three sides to the truth, yours, the other person's, and the truth which is somewhere in the middle. What you feel or think may be full of bias simply because you do not know what the other person has gone through. It is why the above information asks you to assess what may cause the abuser to lash out.

Suggestions one and two will help you on your path to self-healing. The psychologist can offer you methods to address abusive situations when they happen and help you get away from them.

Take some time to decide what you hope for in your parental relationship with an abusive parent or parents. Do you want to keep this person in your life? Is this relationship worth the emotional turmoil that they cause? Are you able to limit your relationship in a way that minimizes the negative effect they have, or even better, enforce boundaries with them that can aid in maintaining your emotional health?

This can be a tough call. For children raised before the last ten to twenty years, it has been ingrained into them to never forget their parents. It is often seen as socially unacceptable to cut a parent out of one's life, no matter how abusive.

But, you can and should do this if it is healthier for you. The downside is you need to be ready to take action and cut those ties and realize that your behavior can be a part of the cycle. If you let fear, anxiety or acceptance of the behavior rule your actions—you will not escape.

Option 1: Limit the time you spend with the person. Stand up for yourself, set boundaries, and be prepared to leave if the abusive behavior continues.

Option 2: Avoid the person. Until you can accept the reasons for their behavior, dismiss them, and remember you are worthwhile and worth loving.

Writing in a journal, telling yourself in the mirror that you feel happy, you feel healthy, and you feel terrific (the famous PMA mantra by Clement Stone), and surrounding yourself with friends who help bolster your confidence are all tasks you should begin, right away. It may seem silly to do these things, but they really help tremendously if you commit to doing them on a regular basis.

Over time, you can retrain your brain to adopt new ways of thinking, to see yourself as worth loving, even if your parent or parents are troubled due to their own inner demons and were unable to make you feel loved.

Chapter 3: Strict Parenting vs. Emotional Abuse

At this point, all the talk of abuse and control probably has you wondering where strict parenting fits into the picture and where the line between discipline and abuse is drawn. Indeed, this topic has been the object of a heated debate for decades now, and lines can get very blurry depending on whom you ask. The perspective can also vary greatly between different cultures in the world, but we will focus on contemporary attitudes in the Western world and other similar places.

First and foremost, it is indisputable that discipline is an integral part of a strong character and has many virtues when it comes to parenting as well. This is how children learn wrong from right early on before their natural empathy and other crucial human emotions are fully developed. To properly and positively discipline a child is also to instill in them a work ethic, sense of morality, strong values, and respect for rules. What's more, a well-disciplined child will be safer out in the world, which will also bolster the parent's trust in them.

The definition of strict parenting can vary from one family to the next, even in the same neighborhood, let alone across the country or the whole world. What everyone can agree on, however, is that rules and discipline require control and, as such, a dose of strictness. The definition of strict parenting is not important, though. What matters much more is for us to identify when strictness treads into abusive territory.

Apart from beatings and other harsh, physical punishments, of course, another area of interest are other forms of disciplining a child, setting boundaries, and teaching lessons without physical contact. These measures can include verbal reprimands, withholding of allowance, grounding, and many other approaches traditionally used by parents.

Strict parenting may sometimes consist of ensuring that a child is kept in a rigid, well-established daily routine and schedule relating to most daily activities. Giving children structure in this way will generally be considered strict parenting, yet it's not abusive. Discipline turns abusive when punishment and consequences for infractions become excessive, inconsistent, and focused on promoting fear rather than a positive lesson. The following examples and explanations will help you determine whether or not you were abused by strict parents.

Abusive parents will put little thought into how they reprimand their child and the punishments they inflict will appear to be on a whim. Rather than explain to the child what they did wrong, these punishments will resemble outbursts and little more than deprivation or psychological torture. The hallmark of an abusive home environment is unpredictability.

If you were properly disciplined by your parents, it meant that you understood all of the rules around the house with perfect clarity. Not only should the rules be clear, but the consequences for every infraction should be well laid out as well. If parents decide to punish their child for failing a test at school, for instance, it should be clear well in advance what kind of consequence this yields. Much more importantly, however, there should be an established reward system for each good result the child brings home.

As such, a healthy home environment where positive discipline is employed will entail a clear set of rules, reward-based incentive, and appropriate, fitting punishments, although punishment quickly becomes redundant once a solid reward system is in place. Any number of rules can thus exist around the house and the upbringing might be very strict, yet there is nothing abusive about it.

On the other hand, an abusive parent will "improvise" and show great inconsistency. A failed test might go completely ignored one day if a parent is in a good mood or preoccupied with something else while, on another day, it can result in you being called worthless, an idiot, or denied a significant portion of your allowance. In extreme cases, an unexpected beating may occur as well.

As you can see, the difference between abusive and competent but strict parents is in that the latter has a plan, a goal, knows what they are doing, and, above all else, leads by example. Such parents are positive role models and they will strictly and personally adhere to the rules that they set for their kids. In contrast, abusive parents frequently don't even follow their own rules. To them, authority is enough, even if they show no responsibility.

Chapter 4: Relationship Abuse: Spouses

Your parental or other familial relationships are not the only relationships where abuse can exist. A spouse, boyfriend, or others you hang around can be just as abusive as those who you are conditioned to believe should love you because you are biologically related.

To some people, the vow of marriage is unbreakable, even when the relationship turns abusive. Over time, the victim gets sucked into the cycle and feels they deserve the trauma.

Make no mistake: **Men can be abused too**, not just women. We tend to emphasize women being abused, in TV and movies. Getting help for truly abused women is important. But, the one thing we never seem to reveal is how men are also susceptible to being emotionally abused, often by women. Yes, in pop culture we may see examples of men being abused by their mothers, but there are fewer examples of how female spouses can abuse their husbands just as easily. It conditions us as a society to believe men are strong and never bullied, and yet it happens more often than you know.

In fact, around 48% of men surveyed in 2010 by the National Center for Injury Prevention and Control reported being psychologically or emotionally abused in their relationships. However, it's important to keep in mind that emotional abuse of a man by a woman is even more stigmatized than physical abuse. The average man is much more likely to report being hurt by a punch or a slap than by words or psychological terror. As such, the figures could be much higher in reality.

This abuse can be manifested in many ways, many of which are very similar to how abusive men mistreat their wives, but some can be female-specific or at least more common. In general, abusive women will regularly insult, belittle, and humiliate their partners, especially in front of other people. A man's masculinity is under direct attack in these instances, and the abuser usually knows what she is doing and aims to destroy the man's image. Much like men, abusive women will manipulate their husbands and try to instill a deep sense of guilt in them, especially concerning the abuse itself.

Of course, another characteristic of abusive women is a strong desire to control their partner at all times. They will try to constantly keep track of their husband's whereabouts to extreme lengths, which is usually accompanied by outbursts of paranoia and accusations of infidelity. This extreme form of jealousy also makes abusive wives try to destroy the husband's relationships with friends, colleagues, and even family. If possible, abusive wives will also exert control through finances.

When it comes to more female-specific forms of spousal abuse, abusive women will sometimes use sex as a weapon of control. In extreme cases, women might threaten their abused husbands and especially boyfriends with accusations of rape, which, of course, is every man's worst nightmare.

This is not at all meant to lessen the trauma that female victims suffer, but rather to add to the truth that emotional abuse can happen to anyone. You just have to be unlucky enough to have an emotionally abusive person in your life. Anyone - a child, adult, or elder - can be emotionally abused.

In marriage, it usually starts with one spouse trying to make life a little easier, less contentious, and thus they end up isolating themselves to make their spouses happy. Eventually, the fights, the verbal abuse, and isolation become a cycle.

In addition to common forms of exerting control, men are much more capable of inflicting specific kinds of emotional abuse on their wives. That especially relates to threats of violence and the use of fear. The situation is especially grim if physical violence did occur in the past on at least one occasion. Once an abusive husband has demonstrated that he is prepared to use violence, mere threats can continue the cycle of terror and lead to a lifetime of walking on eggshells for the victim. That isn't to say that abusive men don't use most of the means we already mentioned. They too will withhold affection, humiliate or belittle their partner, and try to control their relationships outside the marriage. These abusive behaviors are common for both sexes and they can go on for years.

It is only when one spouse moves on or gets pushed to the point they might have an affair, that they may realize the trauma that has occurred. It takes time, friends, and family to help someone get through the healing process.

The Cause

The cause of spousal abuse is often a broken home, which leads the spouse to suffer from a psychological disorder. This is not an absolute truth, but it is a common reason. If you are the type of person to put up with the abuse because you made vows, and you allow control to slip through your fingers, you are also part of the cause which allows this behavior to continue.

It is not your fault, and you should make sure you instill that truth into your mind, but you can make a conscious choice about whether or not you choose to accept the situation you are in. It can be so easy to become complacent in life, to just accept what is happening to you and believe you have no means of changing your life. But you have the power to stop your abuser from victimizing you, even after they are long out of your life.

If you do not already know what causes or caused your abuser to victimize you—try and find out. Most spouses show signs if they were abused as children, even if they are unwilling to discuss it. A major sign is a disinterest in keeping in touch with their family. They do not invite you to meet their family and are extremely tense when family members are around. You can also pick up on continuing abuse, such as derogatory language, when you are with their family.

However, keep in mind that just because there is a reason they are abusive to you, does not mean that it is acceptable to abuse you, or even worse-to allow your spouse to abuse your children. Their upbringing is never an excuse, but if there is a reason why they are this way, perhaps there is a way that they can heal and stop their abusive behaviors. This is ONLY if they are willing to get professional help, and have strategies in place and are willing to accept constructive feedback on healing. Be wary of abusers who promise to change and just suck you right back into the cycle of abuse. Set a limit for how much you will accept, and stick to it. Be knowledgeable on common tactics of manipulation, such as guilting, gaslighting, or threatening suicide.

Once you know the cause, you can begin to heal.

Exercises to Heal

1. Seek professional help.

2. Find ways to contact your family and friends when your spouse is not around.

3. Stop giving in simply to keep the status quo.

4. Decide if you want to stay and continue the abuse or escape for your health. If there are children involved, consider how the abuse affects them. Are they safe and healthy if there is abuse in the household?

5. Write your feelings in a journal.

6. When the cycle of abuse begins, log what triggered it, and accept that there is rarely a way to avoid it. Now record five ways you can change your reaction.

Your reaction is not one that must be toward the person. You do not have to do anything but remain silent in front of your spouse and accept their behavior as you have in the past. However, what you do when you are out of their sight and to help yourself heal is for you alone.

The reactions are meant to be internal. When someone calls you a loser, you think of five reasons you are not. When you are blamed for your spouse's misdeeds, you will have five things that discount those items as they are spoken in your mind.

Anger is often a reaction a free spouse feels after escaping abuse. How do they deal with that anger, even depression? First, you may need medication to handle the depression. Second, find support among family and friends who do not judge, but listen. Third, understand the abusive nature, accept it is a disorder, and **decide** you are not going to let it affect your day. No matter how many times a day the abuse happens or how long it continues or continued—decide you cannot change the person, you can only change yourself and your outlook on life to be happier and healthier.

Acknowledge the hurt, why it hurts, and then put it in a box and let it go. It is okay if things resurge every now and again. However, to let it rule your everyday life means you are still letting yourself be a victim. You have the power to stop it.

Every time a setback occurs, you say "no,"-out loud if you need to: use your coping mechanisms and keep going.

Emotional Abuse in Other Relationships

Boyfriends, girlfriends and any friend may cause you to suffer from abuse. At first, it is difficult to notice it, but then something in your relationship changes. It becomes clear that the abuse is occurring.

Like the above exercises and tips, when you recognize the victimization you have suffered, it is time to deal with it. Accept that setbacks may happen, and plan out how to prevent falling into abusive situations in the future, and build resolve.

When it comes to friendships, many people underestimate just how damaging the abusive among these relationships can be for certain folks. This is because friendships are seen as something that can be disposed of much more easily than marriage, for instance. True friends are becoming increasingly rare and are replaced by a wide circle of acquaintances instead. As such, we all know that friendship isn't something that can be found around the corner and that it can take years to build it.

This is why misinterpreting an abusive relationship for a true friendship can be so dangerous. In an attempt to cherish a friendship, you can end up holding on to someone who just uses you for their selfish gain, sabotages you, or outright verbally abuses you, especially when other friends are around. They will treat you well when they need something from you, but things change dramatically as soon as you're not useful to them. Such a tainted friendship can befall many people, especially those who are reserved and haven't had much social experience in the past.

It's important to understand that just because you might not be particularly socially active doesn't mean that you should settle for any person calling him or herself a friend. On top of that, the fundamental truth of life is that it's better to be alone than commit yourself to people who abuse you. It might be difficult to swallow, but it's a recipe for success because once you stop degrading yourself to accommodate people who don't care about you, you will begin to attract those who appreciate the person you really are. This is how true friends come along most of the time, and even if they don't, at least you won't be abused.

Chapter 5: Further Tips and Exercises to Help

The previous chapters might sound like healing from a trauma relating to emotional abuse from a parent or in a relationship is easy. It is not. It takes time, and also requires you to change your mindset.

You have taken the first steps by reading material about emotional abuse. You can now categorize it and consider what causes it to happen by looking at the abuser's perspective.

Now, it is time for you to realize that a change in your life is required. How are you going to feel if those around you view you as less than you are? A victim may slip into thinking this is the case. A healed individual realizes an important truth: "It does not matter how others view you, but rather what you think of yourself."

A woman, working in the same field for over five years, is still viewed as less than she was because her job while requiring a great deal of hard work, does not pay a lot. At first, it bothered her when her family thought less of her and felt that she could do more. She was not respected and felt like a burden on her immediate family because she believed she was what her extended family perceived her as.

How was she able to move on? It may not have been long-standing abuse or what you suffer from, but the moral still applies. This woman valued herself. She looked at what she accomplished, repeated to herself that no one else in her family could do what she was doing, and she was also helping her immediate family in other ways.

Whenever her extended family made her feel less than she was, this young girl examined her strengths. Her job as a consultant meant she could take care of her ailing father, drop everything and help her brother with his kids as a live-in nanny, and there was and still is value in that.

Take out a piece of paper.

Write down at least one thing you have done that makes you valuable. It can be how valued you are at work, bringing a child into the world, or anything else, no matter how small you may consider it to be. You have at least one thing you can be proud of.

Now think of a second and a third. Each time someone belittles you or the abuser tries to bring you back into the cycle—think of the value you have. Your confidence will build. Eventually, you will create a new cycle where you instantly think of your value and realize one morning that you have changed.

You will understand you are no longer a victim, but a healthy adult, who suffered at some point and grew stronger because of it. When doubts come creeping back into your mind, you can block them with positivity.

If you happen to be a victim of abuse that was inflicted a long time ago by someone who is long-gone but has left you with deep scars, you might also have a fair bit of anger bottled up inside. You should understand that this is okay, as anger is a very human feeling, especially when you have suffered injustice so undeservingly. Letting go of anger can sometimes be very difficult or next to impossible, which is also okay.

The thing about anger is that if you can't dispose of it, you can make it work for you. Think of it as an unused source of energy that is currently eating away at you instead of being put to good use. This is something you can and should change. Anger can be a very potent source of motivation to do better and achieve great things, particularly when it's directed at someone who you feel vindictive toward. There is hardly a better way of getting revenge against those who hurt, belittled, and abused you than living a prosperous life as a healthy and fulfilled individual.

This might be unorthodox advice, as we are frequently thought to suppress or dispose of negative feelings. Sometimes, though, it's much better to channel and harness these emotions in a productive way than to try and eliminate them, especially with medication. Medication is certainly necessary at times, but being too quick to turn to the pills for help can leave you just suppressing the symptoms instead of treating the problem.

You should start thinking positively and focus on what you want to achieve in life instead of dwelling on all the ways in which you have been emotionally incapacitated. Focusing on your pain too hard can turn you into a prisoner who would rather stay locked in than break out because always looking at the negative side has a way of wearing a person down and keeping them stuck.

If you remember only one thing from the above—it should be this—It takes more energy to keep thinking negatively than it does to be positive.

1. Take care of yourself.

2. Let the anger come.

3. Seek help when you need it.

4. Avoid your abuser, and only speak to them if you absolutely must, such as for the benefit of your children if you have them.

5. Act. You have done your research, now follow through.

6. Re-build your self-esteem with the tips provided and other measures you discover.

If you can follow the above six tips, you will begin to heal further. Also, seek out support groups if you are the type to like being in social situations. Other people who suffer from emotional abuse can help you to build confidence, listen to you, and support you because they know what you have been through or are going through.

In general, you will be at a great advantage on your road to recovery if you are not alone. Perhaps more important than just feeling less lonely and isolated is the fact that an outside perspective can do wonders to help you understand yourself and your pain better, especially if you are still unsure of whether or not you have been abused.

Support groups are great because they provide you with people you can relate to and share experiences with, but, sometimes, the input from those who have had no personal experience with emotional or any other kind of abuse can be invaluable. It might seem counterintuitive, but the truth is that victims of abuse can find it difficult to be impartial, especially if the abuse is ongoing.

Apart from therapists who are professionals at identifying problems of this nature, regular folks whom you trust and who have had a very normal life and upbringing can help you in connecting the dots and understanding your experience better.

People who have stable, healthy lives and relationships can be remarkably effective in pointing out what is and isn't normal.

This is especially true if you think you might be having problems in your marriage but don't want to jump to conclusions. If for whatever reason, it's not possible to talk about it with your spouse, you can try to confide in a trustworthy friend, acquaintance, or relative who you know has a healthy marriage. Explain to them your uncertainties and what you think might be wrong, and you will garner valuable outside information to use as reference before you decide to go to a therapist or other professional.

Conclusion

Thank you again for downloading this book!

I hope this book was able to help you to understand you are not alone, and there is help. You can heal from your emotional abuse by facing the person, avoiding the person, and finding methods of coping. It takes time, so give yourself what you need. Allow setbacks to occur and go through the stages of grief. You will be in denial, angry, sad and, eventually, you will be able to heal as you realize the relationship you lost was not worth keeping.

The next step is to use the exercises in the above pages, fall back on the tips as much as you need to, and let yourself see yourself for the bright, intelligent person you have always been.

Support is necessary, whether it is from healthy relationships or therapy sessions. You can take a step to join support groups with others who were emotionally abused or seek relaxation, solitude and a way to take care of yourself to feel better about who you are.

No one has the right to abuse you, and when it happens slowly over time, you may not realize what has occurred. But, you are now on the path to healing. You have methods to get in a better place by loving yourself before you begin to love others again. Start your journey by concentrating on you.

If this helped you, I hope you can take some time to leave a review for this book on Amazon!

Go to **https://tinyurl.com/yczdev8b**

Thank You

Thank you and good luck!

Thank you and good luck! Free eBook on the next page!

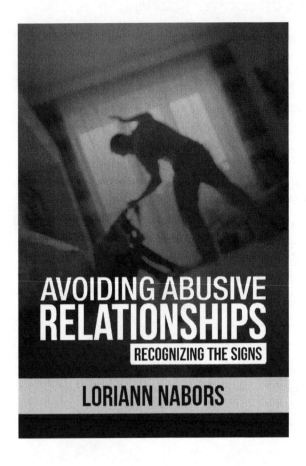

⇨ To   get   your   Free   EBook,   go   to:
https://tinyurl.com/y7yzfmmm

More additional information for free!

You are about to Discover:

- Avoiding Abusive Relationships

- Dating Abuse Is Not A Loving Relationship

- Dating Abuse - Types of Dating Abuse

- Dating Violence - Important Information

- Dealing With A Stalker

- Don't Pick Up a Stalker Online

- Emotional Blackmail in a Relationship

- Emotional Blackmail

- Mending the Rift

- How Can You Tell If You Are In A Toxic Relationship

- Is Your Toxic Relationship Driving You Nuts?

- Knowing The Signs Of A Dangerous Relationship

- On Line Dating Dangers-You Cant Be Too Careful

- Recognizing An Abusive Relationship

- Teenage Relationship Abuse-Growing Problem Among Teens

- And much, much more!

⇨ To get your Free EBook, go to: **https://tinyurl.com/y7yzfmmm**

Search on Amazon: anxiety andrew

Made in the USA
San Bernardino, CA
24 January 2019